baby bullet

user manual and cookbook

baby bullet.

Make an entire week's worth of all natural baby food in less than 5 minutes!

IMPORTANT SAFEGUARDS AND CAUTIONARY INFORMATION
SAVE THESE INSTRUCTIONS

FOR YOUR SAFETY, CAREFULLY READ ALL INSTRUCTIONS BEFORE OPERATING YOUR BABY BULLET.

When using electrical appliances, basic safety precautions should always be followed including the following:

- To avoid risk of electrical shock, never immerse the cord, plug or *Power Base* in water or other liquids.

- This appliance has a polarized plug (one prong is wider than the other). To reduce the risk of electric shock, this plug will only fit in a polarized outlet one way. If the plug does not fit easily into the outlet, reverse the plug. If it still does not fit, contact a qualified electrician. **Do not modify the plug or outlet in any way**.

- The use of attachments not recommended or sold by the manufacturer may cause fire, electric shock or injury.

- The use of attachments, including canning jars, not recommended by the manufacturer may cause a risk of injury to persons.

- Unplug the Baby Bullet when it is not in use, before putting on or taking off parts, and before cleaning or assembling.

- Do not pull or twist the power cord.

- Do not allow the cord to dangle over the edge of a counter or table.

- Do not allow the cord to touch hot surfaces such as the stove.

- Periodically inspect the cord and plug for damage. Do not operate any appliance with a damaged cord or plug, if the appliance malfunctions, or is dropped or damaged in any manner. If damaged, contact Customer Service for assistance in obtaining a replacement.

- Keep hands and utensils away from the blade while chopping or blending food to reduce the risk of severe injury or damage to the unit. A scraper may be used to move food around, but only when the unit is not running.

- Avoid Contacting moving parts.

visit us on facebook

- Never let the motor run for more than one minute at a time as it can cause permanent damage. If the motor stops working, unplug the Power Base and let it cool for a few hours before attempting to use it again. Your Baby Bullet has an internal thermal breaker that shuts off the unit if it overheats. The Power Base will reset when the thermal breaker cools down.
- Always use your Baby Bullet on a clean, flat, hard, dry surface.
- Do not blend hot liquids in the short cup or any closed top container.
- Never blend carbonated beverages. Released gases can cause pressure to build up and the container to burst, resulting in possible injury.
- Make sure the blade base is securely screwed onto the Short Cup or Batchbowl before placing it on the Power Base.
- Never leave the Baby Bullet unattended while it is in use.
- Close supervision is necessary when any appliance is used near children.
- To reduce the risk of injury, be certain that the blade is completely and firmly screwed on to the Short Cup or Batchbowl container before operating the appliance.
- Do not use the Baby Bullet outdoors.
- Blades are sharp. **Handle carefully.**
- Check gasket to make sure it is completely seated in the Baby Blend Blade or Milling Blade base before each use.
- Do not attempt to defeat the cover interlock mechanism.

BATCHBOWL SAFEGUARDS

- Always operate the Batchbowl with the Lid firmly in place.
- Never blend carbonated beverages. Released gases can cause pressure to build up and the container to burst, resulting in possible injury.
- When blending hot liquids, remove center piece of two-piece cover.
- Always ensure that the two-piece cover is firmly in place before operating the appliance.
- Never insert food into the Batchbowl by hand while the Baby Bullet is running. Remove the Batchbowl from the Power Base to add ingredients.

IMPORTANT MICROWAVE SAFEGUARDS

- **WE NEVER RECOMMEND MICROWAVING BABY FOOD!**
- The Baby Bullet is completely **BPA-free!**
- Microwaving food could result in hot spots that can burn Baby's mouth. Always check the temperature throughout and stir any heated food before serving.
- Never heat foods for longer than 2 minutes consecutively: Heat for 2 minutes. Let the food sit for 2 minutes, then heat for another 2 minutes if necessary.
- Do not blend hot liquids in the Short Cup or any closed top container.
- Never microwave with the blade or lid attached.
- When microwaving, beware of steam and use an oven mitt to remove hot cups or containers from the microwave.
- Follow the precautions, heating times and recommendations found in your microwave oven instruction manuals.
- Do not overcook food.
- Some products, such as whole eggs, may explode in the mircowave and should not be heated using the Baby Bullet cups.
- Do not use excessive time when heating water or other liquids in the microwave.
- **Superheated Water** – Liquids such as water or soups are able to become over-heated beyond the boiling point without appearing to be boiling. Visible bubbling or boiling when the container is removed from the microwave is not always present. **This could result in very hot liquids suddenly boiling over when a spoon or other utensil (such as the Baby Bullet blade) is inserted into the liquid. To reduce the risk of injury to persons:**
  – Do not overheat liquid.
  – Stir liquid both before and halfway through heating it to avoid eruption.
  – After heating, allow the container to stand in the microwave for a short time before removing the container.
  – Use extreme care when inserting a spoon or any other utensil into the container.
  – Hot food and/or steam can cause burns. Be careful when opening the Baby Bullet cups when they contain hot foods or liquids.
  – To prevent possible injury, always use protective oven gloves and direct steam away from hands and face.

<u>SAVE THESE INSTRUCTIONS</u>
<u>FOR HOUSEHOLD USE ONLY</u>

visit us on facebook f

Table of Contents

Table of Contents

visit us on facebook

Table of Contents

The Baby Bullet System

We are proud to introduce the latest member of the Magic Bullet family – the Baby Bullet! The Baby Bullet has all the power and convenience of the original Magic Bullet and so much more! Specifically **designed to make healthy, nutritious baby food in just seconds. In fact, you can create and store a week's worth of baby food in less than 5 minutes!** The Baby Bullet system is, hands down, the most convenient in baby food making for quality, efficiency and affordability.

With the Baby Bullet, in less time than it takes to go to the store and buy one jar of food, you can create 7 flavors of delicious, preservative free baby food using the finest organic ingredients. And guess what? You'll actually be **saving money by going organic!** One organic sweet potato costs about $1.20 and will make about 10 ounces of homemade baby food. That's only 12 cents per serving for what costs about $1 in a jar. And when you make your own baby food, you know EXACTLY what is going in it…fresh, wholesome foods and nothing else!

The best thing about the Baby Bullet Baby Food Making System is that it gives you both the tools and the information you need to **set the stage for a lifetime of healthy eating.** From identifying the signs that Baby is ready to try solids, to how to choose the perfect, freshest produce, to tips for storage… **the Baby Bullet will be with you every step of the way.**

baby bullet

Why Homemade?

Babies typically triple their weight in the first year. So, if we are what we eat, it's our job to make sure Baby's food is fresh and healthy!

With the Baby Bullet, creating homemade food for your baby is a faster, healthier, less expensive alternative to buying overpriced, over processed jarred baby food.

Until now, jarred baby food has been considered the most convenient way to feed your growing baby, but now with the Baby Bullet, you can **make 7 days worth of wholesome, homemade baby food in less than 5 minutes.** That's less time than it takes to find your keys, put the stroller in the trunk and get the baby in the car! And jarred food is up to <u>10 times</u> more expensive than homemade baby food.

It's well known that homemade baby food is more nutritious than commercially prepared baby food because it is fresher and much less processed, but a lesser known, yet highly disturbing fact is **that jarred baby food has a shelf life of up to 3 years**. What?? You wouldn't feed your baby a 3 year old banana, so why is it okay to feed your sweet cherub 3 year old banana baby food? How <u>fresh</u> can a banana be that's been sitting on a shelf for 3 years?

Even when jarred food is labeled both preservative free and organic, the reason it <u>can</u> have a shelf life of 3 years is because it's been heated to such an enormous degree that no bacteria can survive in it. But guess what – **vitamins and minerals can't survive in that kind of heat either!** So, most of the nutrition has been leached out of jarred food during that preservation process.

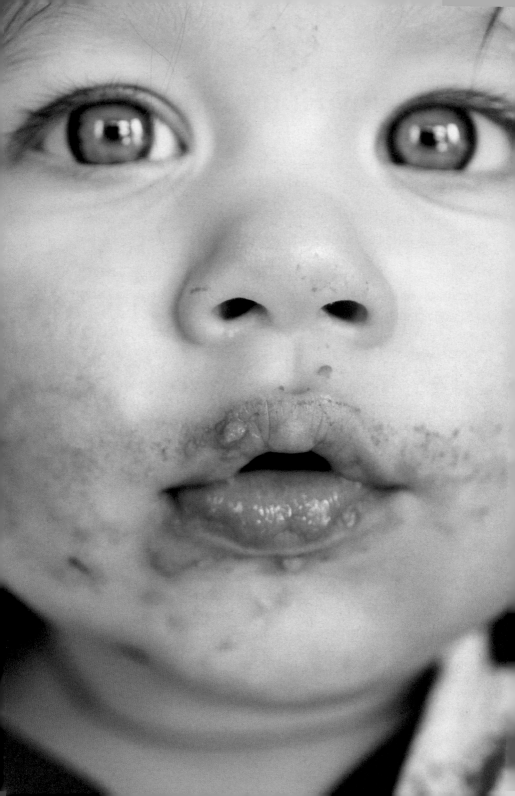

The Darker Side of Jar Food

Plus, did you know there is a certain level of acceptable "non-food" ingredients that can turn up in your jarred baby food? Guess what kinds of thing these "non-foods" include? Bug parts, rodent hairs, rodent droppings and more. DISGUSTING! These non-food ingredients are an acceptable standard in the food processing industry, but it's quite a bit different when you think about them being fed to YOUR tiny baby.

The bottom line is, jarred food is convenience food. It's full of fillers, preservatives, additives and sweeteners. And just as adults shouldn't eat every meal from a drive-thru, can or box, it's not healthy for babies and toddlers to consume processed, packaged baby foods more than on rare occasions. JARRED FOOD SHOULD BE THE EXCEPTION, NOT THE NORM FOR FEEDING YOUR BABY.

The good news is, the Baby Bullet makes it easier than ever to create healthy, nutritious baby food in just seconds... and for just pennies!

Food Made With Love

When you make your own baby food – you know EXACTLY what is going into each meal because you pick the ingredients! No starchy fillers, no hidden salt or sugar, no scary "non-food" surprises… just your hand picked ingredients and your baby's favorite flavor combinations made with love. Now that's the safest way to feed your baby!

Introducing the Baby Bullet Baby Food Making System

What You Get

For Preparing

Spatula

Batchbowl

Short Cup

Power Base

Milling Blade

Baby Blend Blade

User Manual and Cookbook

Pocket Nutritionist

For Storing

Stay-fresh Resealable Lid

Batch Tray

6 Date-Dial Storage Cups

Tray

There Are Four Components in the Baby Bullet Baby Food Making System

① Planning

When it comes to great nutrition – an ounce of planning is worth its weight in gold! That's why the Baby Bullet Baby Food Making System comes with two invaluable planning tools.

The Pocket Nutritionist

The "magic" behind the Baby Bullet Baby Food Making System starts with your handy in-store companion, the *"Pocket Nutritionist"* which teaches parents:

- Which foods to avoid in the first year
- Which foods should be organic
- How to choose a well rounded weekly menu
- How to select the freshest produce
- Exactly how much produce to buy to meet your baby's needs
- The health benefits associated with the foods your baby eats
- And more!

This amazingly informative guide will help you navigate the grocery store aisles for exactly the right foods for your child at any age. This pocket-sized guide saves you time and money – every time you shop! NEVER LEAVE HOME WITHOUT IT!

visit us on facebook

The Baby Bullet User Manual and Cookbook*

This wonderfully comprehensive, easy to follow book contains everything you need to know about operating the Baby Bullet and feeding your child for the first 18 months.

The book includes:
- The signs that Baby is ready to start on solids
- The "No-No" Food List for the first year
- A Step-By-Step plan for Baby's first meal
- The proper schedule for introducing new foods
- Eating schedules for each stage of development
- Wholesome recipes!
- A food journal for tracking favorites and reactions to foods
- How to choose a well rounded weekly menu
- And much, much more!

The *Baby Bullet User Manual and Cookbook* also includes the very important *Baby Bullet Food Journal* which helps you track your baby's reactions as you introduce new foods. From a simple "yuck" to an allergic reaction, you have a place to note every single thing that your baby eats and exactly what happens at each meal and after each meal, so you'll know what agrees with Baby and what doesn't.

The information contained in our guide and cookbook is not a substitute to regular baby care. Always consult your pediatrician regarding nutrition and the feeding of your child.

❷ Preparing

Follow the eating schedule and choose your favorite recipes for your **Stage One** Perfect Purées, **Stage Two** Tasty Textures and in about 5 minutes you can whip up a week's worth of your child's favorites.

The Batchbowl
The larger vessel, the *Batchbowl*, is for creating large amounts of baby food for storing. The *Batchbowl* is **BPA-free** and dishwasher safe (top shelf only). *Never operate without the cover on.*

 ### The Short Cup
This cup is used to mix and store your ingredients. It is **BPA-free** and dishwasher-safe (top shelf only).

The Power Base
The *Power Base* is the heart of the *Baby Bullet* system. Simply place either the *Batchbowl* or the *Short Cup* on to the *High-Torque Power Base*, press down and twist…it couldn't be easier!

CAUTION!

- **Do not submerge the Power Base in water and always unplug the Power Base before cleaning it.**
- **Always make sure the cover is on the Batchbowl when using.**
- **Keep hands and utensils away from the cutting blade while chopping or blending food to reduce the risk of severe injury to person or damage to the blender.**

The Blades
The Baby Bullet comes with two blades:

 The *Baby Blend Blade* is for puréeing and blending foods.

 The *Milling Blade* is for milling grains to make cereals. **Note:** The *Milling Blade* is only used on the *Short Cup*.

Both blades are **BPA-free** and dishwasher-safe.

Note: In the base of the blades there is a plastic gasket that creates an airtight seal with the Baby Bullet vessels. After washing a blade, check to make sure the gasket is still inside as the heat from some dishwashers can cause them to become loose.

❸ Storage

It's on to storage where <u>you</u> decide whether to freeze or re-frigerate your fabulous concoctions. The good news is that the Baby Bullet comes with our exclusive *Date-Dial Lids!* So you can spoon fresh baby food right into the *Storage Cups* and twist on the *Date-Dial Lid* to track when the baby food was created. Then, either freeze or refrigerate!

Or, when you are making large batches of baby food, use the *Baby Bullet Soft Tip Spatula* to spoon purées right into the handy *Batch Tray*. Cover and freeze, then either pop them out as you need them, or pop them all out at once and save them in a freezer bag so your *Batch Tray* is ready to freeze even more of Baby's favorites. It's that easy!

> *Note:* **Refrigerated foods need to be enjoyed within 3 days. We recommend consuming frozen foods within 30 days for optimum freshness. For freezing, you can use either the Batch Tray or the Date-Dial Storage Cups.**

The Baby Bullet Storage Tools Include:

Six Storage Cups with Date-Dial Lids
Your Baby Bullet System comes with 6 revolutionary *Date-Dial Storage Cups* that are both refrigerator and freezer friendly. Simply spoon your baby food in, twist on the lid and turn the *Date-Dial* to show the date you created the food. Now you never have to guess when you made the food – you'll know exactly when you made it. The *Date-Dial Storage Cups* are **BPA-free** and dishwasher-safe (top rack only).

visit us on facebook f

The Batch Tray

To save even more time and money, it's easy to make large batches of your baby's favorite foods and freeze them for later use. The *Baby Bullet Batch Tray* is perfect for freezing over 12 ounces of baby food and the **BPA-free** silicone "easy pop" cups make it a breeze to pop out one serving to several servings, or all 6 Baby Bullet servings with ease.

The Soft Tip Spatula

The *Baby Bullet Soft-Tip Spatula* has been specifically designed to get your baby food creations into the Baby Bullet storage vessels with ease. This spatula is dishwasher safe (top shelf only), but can typically be cleaned with just a quick rinse with warm soapy water.

❹ Serving

When it's chow time, serving Baby Bullet baby food couldn't be easier! For refrigerated foods, you can serve right from the storage cup or portion out a serving from the *Short Cup*. **Never save leftovers that have come in to contact with a used or dirty spoon**. Always throw out leftovers!

To defrost frozen foods, either remove the food from the freezer and place into the refrigerator a few hours ahead of mealtime, or place the sealed food (either in a storage cup or in a sealed plastic bag) into a bowl of hot water. If you are in a rush, change the water a few times until the food is defrosted. Otherwise, just leave the food in the hot water and it will take about 20 minutes to defrost.

We do not recommend microwaving baby food as it can create "hot spots" in the food that can burn Baby's mouth.

Using the
Baby Bullet Blender

Making Large Batches of Fruit and Vegetable Purées

ALWAYS use clean hands, clean cooking utensils, clean preparation surface(s), clean pots/pans, etc. when making and preparing homemade baby food. **Cleanliness** is VERY important when making homemade baby food.

1 Twist the *Baby Blend Blade* on to the bottom of the *Batchbowl* for puréeing large batches of baby food.

2 Add very steamed or soft boiled fruits/vegetables into the *Batchbowl* making sure any skins, cores, pits or stems have been removed.

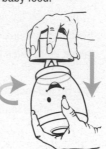

3 Add 1/8 - 1/4 cup of water (you can always add more if you'd like a thinner purée).

4 Place the top onto the *Batchbowl* and twist into place.

5 Place the *Batchbowl* onto the *Power Base*, push down and twist to engage the motor.

6 Blend your food until you've achieved the desired consistency. Use the Pulse Technique (page 29) for creating textured foods.

7 Spoon your purée into the *Date-Dial Storage Cups* to store in either the freezer or the refrigerator. – Don't forget to set your date.

8 Or, for longer term storage, spoon your purée into the *Batch Tray* and freeze.

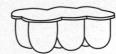

Note: Refrigerated foods must be consumed within 3 days. Frozen foods are good for up to 30 days.

visit us on facebook f

Making Smaller Batches of Fruit and Vegetable Purées

ALWAYS use clean hands, clean cooking utensils, clean preparation surface(s), clean pots/pans, etc. when making and preparing homemade baby food. **Cleanliness** is VERY important when making homemade baby food.

1. Add very steamed or soft boiled fruits/vegetables into the *Short Cup* making sure that any skins, cores, pits or stems have been removed. Let the ingredients cool a bit before blending

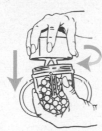

2. Add ¼ cup of water (you can always add more if you'd like a thinner purée).

3. Twist the *Baby Blend Blade* onto the *Short Cup* for puréeing, or twist the *Milling Blade* onto the *Short Cup* for milling.

4. Place the *Short Cup* onto the *Power Base*, push down and twist to engage the motor.

5. Blend your food until you've achieved the desired consistency.

6. Either place into a bowl and serve or spoon your purée into the *Date-Dial Storage Cups* to store in either the freezer or the refrigerator.

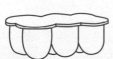

7. For longer term storage, spoon your purée into the *Batch Tray,* snap on the lid and freeze.

Note: Refrigerated foods must be consumed within 3 days. Frozen foods are good for up to 30 days.

visit us on facebook

Milling Grains and Rice For Cereals

Short Cup Milling For Smaller Batches

ALWAYS use clean hands, clean cooking utensils, clean preparation surface(s), clean pots/pans, etc. when making and preparing homemade baby food. **Cleanliness** is VERY important when making homemade baby food.

1 Add the desired amount of rice or grains into the *Short Cup*.

2 Twist on the *Milling Blade*.

3 Place the *Short Cup* onto the *Power Base* and twist to start grinding.

4 Grind until you've achieved a fine powder (see brown rice purée recipe on page 61).

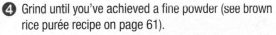

Baby Bullet Techniques

The Pulse Technique

The Pulse Technique comes in handy when Baby is ready for chunkier, more textured fare. Pulsing takes a tiny bit of getting used to, but once you get a feel for it, you'll be a pro in no time! To Pulse, you simply press straight down on the cup very quickly and immediately release.

THE SECRET: The trick to successful Pulsing is to make sure that the machine doesn't accidentally slip into purée mode. To avoid this, use your other hand to apply counter-clockwise pressure as you Pulse

The "Shake" Technique

Sometimes, when you are working with thicker recipes, like Chicken, Brown Rice and Squash (page 78) the density of the mixture can make it hard for the ingredients toward the top of the cup to make it down to the blade.

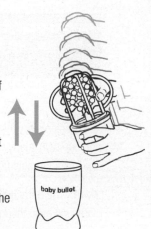

If some of your ingredients are having a hard time making it down to the blade, simply use this Shake technique.

Step 1: Remove the *Batchbowl/Short Cup* assembly from the Power Base... pick it up and shake it like a cocktail shaker.
Step 2: Place the vessel back onto the Power Base.
Step 3: Repeat... if necessary until you achieve the consistency you want.
Note: You may need to add more water to get the right consistency.

Cleaning
The Baby Bullet

Everyone hates cleaning up, which is just one more reason the Baby Bullet is such a wonderful time saver. You can make and cook fresh, homemade baby food from scratch and only use one vessel! Imagine creating tasty purées, wholesome soups and fantastic mini-meals - or turning the family's spaghetti dinner into a delicious meal fit for Baby – with just a single cup and blade to put in the dishwasher! It doesn't get any easier than that!

ALWAYS UNPLUG THE BABY BULLET WHEN CLEANING OR ASSEMBLING.

Washing the Baby Bullet

Cleaning the Baby Bullet is so easy… simply place any of the pieces (except for the Power Base) on the top shelf of the dishwasher or hand wash with warm soapy water and rinse.

ALWAYS MAKE SURE THE GASKETS ARE STILL IN THE BLADE BASE AFTER CLEANING. THE HEAT FROM SOME DISHWASHERS CAN CAUSE THEM TO BECOME LOOSE AND POP OUT.

Stubborn Cleanup

If ingredients dry inside the Baby Bullet, make your clean up a snap by filling the cup with soapy water and microwaving it for one minute. That will loosen the stuck ingredients and with a light scrub, you'll be all done.

Note: The Baby Bullet *Short Cup* and *Date-Dial Storage Cups* are microwave safe, and even though they are BPA-free, we don't advise microwaving baby food in them because microwave heating can create very hot spots that can easily burn Baby's mouth.

WE DO NOT RECOMMEND MICROWAVING BABY FOOD AS IT CAN CREATE "HOT SPOTS" IN THE FOOD THAT CAN BURN BABY'S MOUTH.

visit us on facebook

Cleaning the Baby Bullet Power Base

For the most part the *Power Base* doesn't really get dirty, but if you neglect to twist the blade on to the cup tightly, liquids can leak out and get into the base and activator buttons.

Here's how to clean it up.

    Step 1: The most important thing is to UNPLUG the *Power Base!*

    Step 2: Use a damp rag to wipe down the inside and outside of the *Power Base.*

- **NEVER SUBMERGE THE POWER BASE IN WATER OR PLACE IT IN THE DISHWASHER**

- Never put your hands or utensils near the moving blade and never use your hands or utensils to press the activator buttons down while the *Power Base* is plugged in.

An exclusive offer for
baby bullet families!

Introducing the amazingly comprehensive
baby food making bible...

the **baby bullet** recipe book and nutrition guide

visit us on facebook f

Get <u>even more</u> out of your
baby bullet
with this soup to nuts baby food guide!

✓ Over 100 Nutrient Packed Recipes!

✓ Nutritional Facts for Each Flavor of Baby Food!

✓ Amazing Tips for Finicky Eaters!

✓ The Baking for Baby Section!

✓ Meal Ideas for Up to 3 Years!

✓ Toddler Friendly "Presentation" Tips!

✓ Healthy Dessert Recipes!

✓ Teething Biscuit Recipes... and More!

Visit
www.babybullet.com/bookoffer
or call
1-855-514-MYBB (1-855-514-6922)
to claim <u>your</u> special offer!

Preparing for the Big Day*

The American Academy of Pediatrics states that the best time to start feeding your baby solids is between 4 and 6 months. Some pediatricians even go on to say, the closer to 6 months, the better. Your baby's digestive system is not mature enough to handle solids until the 4th month. This may be even later for preemies. So even though people may suggest feeding your baby earlier, your baby and your pediatrician will let you know when it's time for solids.

Signs That Your Baby Is Ready For Solid Food

Experts all agree that there are obvious signs when your baby is ready to start eating solids. Here is a comprehensive list of those signs. Please remember, even though you may get pressure from others to start your baby on solids, your baby will let you know when the time is right.

- Baby is at least 4 months old but somewhere between 4 and 6 months.
- Baby weighs at least 12-15 pounds and has doubled birth weight.
- Baby can sit upright with support and has the ability to "lean in" for more food.
- Baby can turn away to show that mealtime is over.
- Baby seems very interested in what you are eating.
- Baby seems consistently hungry after nursing or drinking a bottle.
- Baby can swallow food vs. instinctively pushing it out with tongue.
- Baby can bring an object to his/her mouth.

The information contained in our guide and cookbook are not a substitute to regular baby care. Always consult your pediatrician regarding nutrition and the feeding of your child.

What Do I Need?

Vegetable Steamer or a Non-Teflon Pot

Most foods need to be cooked before they can be puréed into baby food except for soft foods like bananas and avocados. Steaming is most often advised because it keeps the nutrients inside the fruits and vegetables. But, boiling is another great alternative. We recommend using the water you boiled your fruits and vegetables in as it adds the vitamins and minerals back into your purée. Let the foods cool down a bit before blending.

High Chair with Tray

Choosing a high chair is an important task. Safety is always first, so stability is the first thing to test on a high chair and the safety strap is second. The strap should prevent Baby from standing or moving around too much in the chair. Then it's on to the tray which should be easy to remove (think one hand) for cleaning and should have a "lip" around the entire tray to keep food and liquids from spilling onto the floor. Comfort is another consideration, so keep that in mind when choosing your high chair and give the padding a once over to see if it's soft and cozy.

Soft Tipped Spoons

Baby's mouth is very sensitive, that's why baby stores are full of different types of spoons designed for Baby's first meals. Take a look at what's out there and decide what you think is right for your little one. It's always safe to grab one or three different spoon styles and then purchase more once you know which ones work to your liking.

Bibs

Very little of Baby's first few meals is going to wind up in Baby's mouth. Most of it will wind up somewhere between Baby's forehead and the floor. If you want to protect Baby's cute little outfit – a bib is a must.

Floor Mat

Which brings us to the floor mat! Much of your baby's fare will end up on the floor. To protect carpet or porous flooring, be sure to get a High Chair Floor Mat. Basically, it's a tarp to throw under Baby's high chair to protect whatever is below.

What is on the Menu?

Allergy Alert

Certain foods have a significantly higher likelihood to cause an allergic reaction in babies – and that's why we've avoided all of those foods! With the Baby Bullet feeding program, we've created a schedule where only the very safest foods are offered to your baby for the first two months of eating solids. Then we introduce some low risk foods and ultimately a full spectrum of healthy foods will be offered in a manner where it's easy to identify any possible allergic reactions so you'll be able to quickly track that back to the culprit. Here is an at-a-glance chart to help you get an overview of what is safe and what is risky.

First Year No-No List

Honey	Raw Strawberries	Whole Milk – as a drink
Peanut Butter	Raspberries and Blackberries	Wheat
Nuts	Corn	Shellfish/Crustaceans
Citrus Fruits	Egg Whites	

- *None of these foods should be consumed in the 1st year without pediatrician approval.*

Hi Risk Allergy Foods

Beans	Mustard	Additives
Legumes	Nuts	*Artificial Foods*
Berries	Onions	
Buckwheat	Papaya	
Cabbage	Peanuts	
Chocolate	Pork	
Cinnamon	Rye	
Citrus Fruit	Semolina	
Coconut	Shellfish	
Corn	Strawberries	
All Dairy	Soybeans	
Egg Whites	Tofu	
Mango	Tomatoes	
Melon	Wheat	
	Yeast	

Low Risk Allergy Foods

Applesauce	Millet
Apricots	Oats
Asparagus	Peaches
Barley	Pears
Beets	Plums
Carrots	Rice
Lettuce	Tapioca

Safest First Foods

Sweet Potatoes	Squash
Avocado	Apples
Brown Rice Cereal	Pears
Peas	Bananas
Zucchini	

visit us on facebook

Signs of an Allergic Reaction

Gas
Diarrhea
Nausea
Vomiting
Stomach Pain
Coughing
Wheezing
Difficulty Breathing
Lip/Face Swelling

Rash
Clear Runny Nose
Itching
Irritability
Fatigue
Eczema
Eye Swelling

Note: Even a small allergic reaction can be the first sign of a severe reaction. Please call your pediatrician at any sign of an allergic reaction!

Prepping for the Big Day!

Tripod with camera perfectly situated ✓
Excited calls to Mom and best friend ✓
High chair ✓
Soft tipped spoon ✓
Super cute bib ✓
Floor mat ✓
Homemade first meal made with love… it's time to make it!

Baby's first meal will be made from one of the foods on this short list:

Banana
Sweet Potato
Pear
Yellow Squash
Zucchini
Green Peas
Apple
Avocado
Brown Rice Cereal

When it's time to choose the <u>very first food that will go into your baby's mouth</u>, suddenly the list seems rather long! Don't fret! Close your eyes and point at this page to choose the first two foods if you have to…because the very first meal will most likely be only about a tablespoon.

Using the ever-important 4-Day Food Introduction Schedule, Baby's first week on solids means only 2 foods will be introduced. Choose your 2 favorites and its almost time to use your Baby Bullet!!

visit us on facebook

Food Chart for Months 4 - 6

Choose from these foods –

1 Avocado = 4 Baby Bullet servings (8 oz)

1 Squash = 10 Baby Bullet servings (20 oz)

1 Banana = 4 Baby Bullet servings (8 oz)

1 Sweet Potato = 10 Baby Bullet servings (20 oz)

1 Cup Peas = 4 Baby Bullet servings (8 oz)

1 Zucchini = 5 Baby Bullet servings (10 oz)

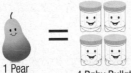

1 Pear = 4 Baby Bullet servings (8 oz)

1 Cup Brown Rice Cereal = 16 Baby Bullet servings (32 oz)

1 Apple = 3 Baby Bullet servings (6 oz)

Note: *Fruit and vegetable sizes vary, so you may wind up with more or less food.*

Making the Right Amount of Food for Week One

For the first week of eating, your baby will have one meal of the same food for the first 4 days. After 4 days, if no signs of allergy have appeared, it's time to switch to food #2 and provide one meal a day of that second food.

For the first week, each meal should not be much more than a tablespoon. Food only keeps for 3 days in the refrigerator, so it's a good idea to fill 4 Storage Cups to the halfway mark with flavor #1 and then 4 Storage Cups to the half way mark with flavor #2. Fill the Batch Tray with any remaining purée and freeze for later use, so you'll have it for backup.

Week One Flavor #1

| Refrigerator | Refrigerator | Freezer | Freezer |

Week One Flavor #2

| Freezer | Freezer | Freezer | Freezer |

Important!! Don't feed baby straight out of the cup unless you are going to finish the contents or throw away any remaining food. You cannot reuse any remaining food as germs and bacteria may have gotten in by way of the spoon.

Now, it's finally time to use the Baby Bullet! The instructions for creating Baby's first purée can be found on pages 52 through 61. You'll be using the *Short Cup* to create Baby's First Foods, so if you need to review the instructions, turn to page 24.

Note: Depending on the two flavors you have chosen...you may have some extra baby food. If so, put the contents in the Batch Tray and freeze for later use.

Storage Reminder! Fresh food keeps in the refrigerator for 3 days. Frozen food keeps for about 30 days.

- **Make sure all sides of the Batch Tray Lid are snapped on and sealed to avoid freezer burn.**

Ready for the Big Day!

You are officially ready! Here are some tips for making Baby's first meal a wonderful experience for both of you.

1. Offer the first meal at a time when Baby isn't too hungry.
2. Offer the first meal early in the day (morning or afternoon) just in case there is a reaction such as gas or colic.
3. Make sure you are in a good mood. Your attitude towards this meal has a lot to do with how this is going to go.
4. Offer food that is a bit warm (think 98.7 degrees) or cool. Don't overheat foods!!
5. The consistency of the food should be almost liquid, it should run off of the spoon. Feel free to add water, formula or breast milk to achieve the right consistency.

Go Time!

At a regularly scheduled AM or midday feeding time, stop halfway through breast feeding or halfway through a bottle and place Baby in the highchair.

Checklist
1) *Baby strapped in high chair.*
2) *Bib on.*
3) *Spoon and clean up towel.*
4) *Protective floor mat.*
5) *The liquid thin food's temperature is somewhere from moderately cool to warm.*
6) *SMILE.*

Feeding Baby

Place a tiny bit of food onto the spoon and put some on Baby's lips. Then place the spoon on the bottom lip and slip the spoon gently into Baby's mouth. This may cause Baby's tongue to push the food back out. If so, use the spoon to scrape the food off of the chin area and try putting it in Baby's mouth again. Repeat.

It the tongue keeps pushing the food back out, don't worry…never push Baby to eat. If the first meal doesn't go well…no worries. Try again in a few days.

Ending Mealtime

A closed mouth, turned head and fussiness are all signs that mealtime is over. If there is food left, throw it out. Never force Baby to continue eating when full. Throw out any leftovers that have come into contact with Baby's mouth or the spoon.

You did it! Congratulations!!! Now jot down ALL the details in the Baby Bullet Journal on page 100.

Week 1

For week one, you will continue to feed Baby one meal a day. After 2 days, make sure you take the servings for day 3 and 4 out of the freezer and place them in the refrigerator to thaw. On day 4, take the servings for day 5 and 6 out of the freezer and place in the refrigerator to thaw.

Week 2

For week 2, you can offer a third flavor, but stay on the 4-Day Food Introduction Schedule, but offer Baby a bit more food than in week one. Offer half of a Baby Bullet serving one time a day, but always watch for Baby to let you know when mealtime is over.

Moving forward

Depending on your baby's age at the time of the first meal, you may be looking at 2 servings a day pretty quickly. Follow Baby's lead. If all meals are being polished off with glee, go ahead and try another meal 3-4 hours after the first one. As Baby gets more used to eating, you will be ready to follow the Stage One Feeding Schedule on page 50.

Stage One - Perfect Purées

Stage One foods start with Baby's first meal and go for the next 6-8 weeks. During Stage One, very simple, low allergy risk ingredients are puréed to a very thin consistency. New foods should be introduced on a 4-day schedule, which means that only one new food is introduced per 4-day period. This is critical for tracking any allergic reactions to a particular food. Use your food journal on page 100 to record what Baby ate, what time, how much and any reactions to the food. (Bowel Movements, cranky, rash, etc).

If you need more journal pages, you can print them out at: www.babybullet.com/journal

Food Chart for Months 4 - 6

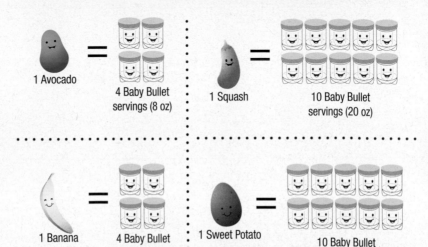

1 Avocado = 4 Baby Bullet servings (8 oz)

1 Squash = 10 Baby Bullet servings (20 oz)

1 Banana = 4 Baby Bullet servings (8 oz)

1 Sweet Potato = 10 Baby Bullet servings (20 oz)

visit us on facebook

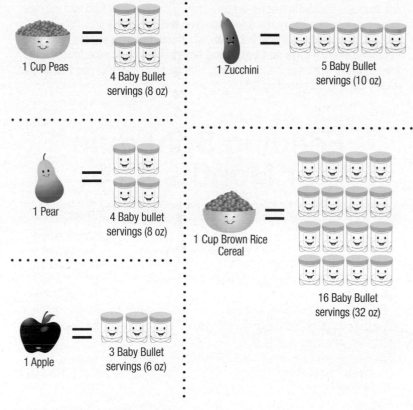

1 Cup Peas	=	4 Baby Bullet servings (8 oz)
1 Zucchini	=	5 Baby Bullet servings (10 oz)
1 Pear	=	4 Baby bullet servings (8 oz)
1 Cup Brown Rice Cereal	=	16 Baby Bullet servings (32 oz)
1 Apple	=	3 Baby Bullet servings (6 oz)

Note: *Fruit and vegetable sizes vary, so you may wind up with more or less food.*

Every child is different, but this chart is a great place to help you start determining your baby's food needs for the day. Remember to start with just one food and stick with that for 4 days. Then, work in a new food and eat only those two foods for the next 4 days and so on and so on until your baby has tried all of the foods on the safest foods list. **Never introduce more than one new food every 4 days and keep good notes about each new food in your food journal.** That way if any rashes or strange poop appears, you'll be able to track it back to the offending food.

Feeding Schedule for Months 4 - 6

Time	Food	Drink
Wake Up Time		Breast/bottle
AM	1/4 to 1 Baby Bullet servings	Breast/bottle
Noon		Breast/bottle
Afternoon	1/4 to 1 Baby Bullet servings	Breast/bottle
PM		Breast/bottle
Bedtime		Breast/bottle

Foods: avocado, brown rice cereal, peas, zucchini, squash, apple, pear, banana, sweet potato.
Food groups: 2 - 4 servings of fruits and vegetables.
1 - 2 servings of cereal.
Food consistency: smooth, thin purée.

Note: Baby will work up to two servings. Start with one and continue until Baby appears to need an additional serving. Do not reuse food that has come in contact with Baby's spoon or mouth! It can contain bacteria.

ALWAYS use clean hands, clean cooking utensils, clean preparation surface(s), pots/pans, etc. when making and preparing homemade baby food. **Cleanliness** is VERY important when making homemade baby food.

The information contained in our guide and cookbook are not a substitute to regular baby care. Always consult your pediatrician regarding nutrition and the feeding of your child.

Preparing Stage One Foods: Perfect Purées

banana purée

Sweet and creamy banana is a delicious, healthy treat for Baby. With notable benefits, including potassium richness and digestive health (helps both constipation and diarrhea!); banana is a perfect and tasty food for Baby.

Baby Blend Blade

Short Cup

1 whole raw banana

¼ cup of water

1 banana yields 8 oz of baby food.

. . . .

1.) Add both ingredients to the *Short Cup*.
2.) Twist on the *Baby Blend Blade*.
3.) Purée until you have achieved the proper smoothness.

 Note – *add less water if you want a thicker food or more water for a thinner purée.*

 10 seconds

sweet potato purée

A global favorite for babies. Sweet potato is a wonderful source of vitamins A, C, B-6 and E! Swcct potato is also a good source of phosphous which supports the growth of healthy bones and teeth. Plus – one sweet potato goes a long way which means lots of delicious baby food for very little effort and $$. Now that's sweet!

Baby Blend Blade   Batchbowl

1 peeled sweet potato boiled or steamed until very soft

1 cup of water

1 sweet potato yields 20 oz of baby food.

. . . .

1.) Twist the *Baby Blend Blade* onto the *Batchbowl*.
2.) Add both ingredients to the *Batchbowl* and secure
     the lid.
3.) Purée until you have achieved the proper smoothness.

 Note – *because sweet potato is so thick and starchy, you may need to use the Pulse Technique on page 29.*

 10 seconds

For more recipes, please visit
www.babybullet.com

zucchini purée

A mild and tasty purée that's chock full of Vitamin C and B6 which support your baby's developing heart and eyes.

Baby Blend Blade   Short Cup

1 zucchini boiled or steamed until soft, then cut

¼ cup of water

1 zucchini yields 10 oz of baby food.

1.) Add both ingredients to the *Short Cup*.
2.) Twist on the *Baby Blend Blade*.
3.) Purée until you have achieved the proper smoothness.

 Note – *add less water if you want a thicker food or more water for a thinner purée.*

 10 seconds

visit us on facebook

pear purée

Sweet and tender, pear makes a divine purée for Baby. Full of fiber, pears are great for "keeping things moving" and folates help Baby's developing brain and spinal cord.

Baby Blend Blade   Short Cup

1 pear boiled or steamed until soft (must be peeled and cored)

¼ cup of water

1 pear yields 8 oz of baby food.

. . . .

1.) Add both ingredients to the *Short Cup*.
2.) Twist on the *Baby Blend Blade*.
3.) Purée until you have achieved the proper smoothness.

 Note – *add less water if you want a thicker food or more water for a thinner purée.*

 10 seconds

green pea purée

Your baby will soon say please when it comes to peas! Delicious and healthy with high levels of Vitamin K, B6 and folic acid...peas are wonderful for growing bones, brains and hearts. Peas are a tried and true baby favorite.

Baby Blend Blade   Short Cup

1 cup of steamed frozen or steamed fresh peas

¼ cup of water

1 cup of peas yields 8 oz of baby food.

. . . .

1.) Add both ingredients to the *Short Cup*.
2.) Twist on the *Baby Blend Blade*.
3.) Purée until you have achieved the proper smoothness.

 Note – *add less water if you want a thicker food or more water for a thinner purée.*

 10 seconds

squash purée

Creamy and mellow, squash is a nutritious and flavorful first meal for Baby. Because of its mild flavor, it's perfect for mixing with other fruit or vegetable purées. Squash supports the development of Baby's eyes, lungs and heart...so bring on the squash!

Baby Blend Blade   Batchbowl

1 yellow squash yields 20 oz of baby food.

1 yellow squash boiled or steamed until soft (with tips removed)

¼ cup of water

. . . .

1.) Twist the *Baby Blend Blade* onto the bottom of the *Batchbowl.*
2.) Add squash and water to the *Batchbowl* and secure the lid.
3.) Purée until you have achieved the proper smoothness.

 Note – *add less water if you want a thicker food or more water for a thinner purée.*

 10 seconds

visit us on facebook

apple purée

Rich with antioxidants, fiber and flavonoids, apples are great for heart health, circulation and digestive health. Always a favorite at any age, puréed apple is a delicious, sweet food that combines well with cereals and vegetables. An apple a day keeps the doctor away!

Baby Blend Blade   Short Cup

1 apple boiled or steamed until soft (must be peeled and cored)

¼ cup of water

1 medium apple yields 6 oz of baby food.

. . . .

1.) Add both ingredients to the *Short Cup*
2.) Twist on the *Baby Blend Blade*.
3.) Purée until you have achieved the proper smoothness.

 Note – *add less water if you want a thicker food or more water for a thinner purée.*

 10 seconds

For more recipes, please visit
www.babybullet.com

avocado purée

Often called the perfect food, avocado is chock full of vitamins, minerals and healthy fats. It's a wonderful super food for a developing baby. Mild and creamy – what's not to like about avocado??

Baby Blend Blade   Short Cup

1 avocado yields 8 oz of baby food.

1 peeled and pitted avocado

¼ cup of water

1.) Add both ingredients to the *Short Cup*.
2.) Twist on the *Baby Blend Blade*
3.) Purée until you have achieved the proper smoothness.

 Note – *to make a thinner purée add more water and blend for a bit longer.*

 10 seconds

visit us on facebook

brown rice cereal

Higher in fiber and nutrition than white rice, brown rice is great for energy and the development of a healthy nervous system. Milled brown rice cereal is a fantastic first food for Baby and combines perfectly with all fruit and vegetable purées.

Milling Blade

Short Cup

1/2 cup of brown rice

4 cups of water

1/2 cup of rice yields 16 oz of baby food.

. . . .

1.) Twist the *Milling Blade* onto the bottom of the *Short Cup*.
2.) Add 1/2 cup of uncooked brown rice to the *Short Cup*.
3.) Twist on the *Milling Blade* and mill to a fine powder.
4.) Add the milled brown rice and 4 cups of water to a pot and cover until it boils. Once it hits a boil, turn down heat to low and cook with cover on for 20 minutes.
5.) Test the consistency of the brown rice cereal – if you want it thinner, add more water.
6.) Once the ideal consistency is achieved. Pour brown rice cereal into storage cups and/or the Batch Tray and refrigerate or freeze.

Note – *This is a great cereal to combine with any fruit or vegetable purée.*

30 seconds

For more recipes, please visit
www.babybullet.com

7 Months!

Continue to feed your little one Perfect Purées on the 4-day Food Introduction Schedule until you've tried all of the foods from the Safest Foods List. Start to mix single flavored fruit or veggie purées with brown rice, millet or oatmeal cereal to keep things interesting. Feel free to combine <u>any</u> of the foods that you've already sampled and <u>know</u> agree with Baby. So, try apple and banana or green beans and yellow squash…mix it up!!

Food Chart for Month 7

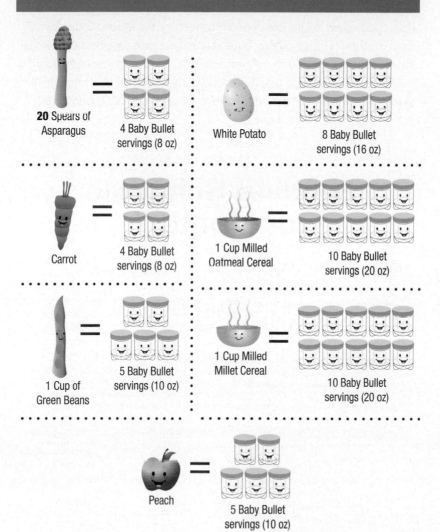

20 Spears of Asparagus = 4 Baby Bullet servings (8 oz)

White Potato = 8 Baby Bullet servings (16 oz)

Carrot = 4 Baby Bullet servings (8 oz)

1 Cup Milled Oatmeal Cereal = 10 Baby Bullet servings (20 oz)

1 Cup of Green Beans = 5 Baby Bullet servings (10 oz)

1 Cup Milled Millet Cereal = 10 Baby Bullet servings (20 oz)

Peach = 5 Baby Bullet servings (10 oz)

Note: *Fruit and vegetable sizes vary, so you may wind up with more or less food.*

Additional Food Possibilities

Cottage Cheese   Tofu   All Natural Plain Yogurt

Many pediatricians like the idea of adding some dairy and tofu into Baby's diet at about 7 months. Cottage cheese, tofu and all natural, plain yogurt are three foods that are easy on growing Baby's digestive system. Check with your pediatrician on whether now is the right time to start adding these foods in. And remember, as with all new foods, use the 4-day Food Introduction Schedule and document all information in your Food Journal.

Feeding Schedule for Month 7

Time	Food	Drink
Wake Up Time	None	Breast/bottle
Breakfast	1 to 1 1/2 Baby Bullet servings	Breast/bottle
Lunch	1 to 1 1/2 Baby Bullet servings	Breast/bottle
Dinner	1 to 1 1/2 Baby Bullet servings	Breast/bottle
Bedtime	None	Breast/bottle

Foods: avocado, brown rice cereal, peas, zucchini, squash, apple, pear, banana, sweet potato, asparagus, carrots, green beans, white potato, peach, tofu, cottage cheese, milled oatmeal cereal, milled millet cereal

Food groups: 3 - 4 servings of fruits and vegetables. 1 - 3 servings of cereal. 1/2 serving of dairy.
Food consistency: Smooth purée (a little less water than last month).

Stage One: Perfect Combo Purées

combo purées

Combine your favorite two purées into one flavor extravaganza. Mix fruits and veggies together for tasty delights. Always use the 4-Day Food Introduction Schedule when introducing new foods.

Baby Blend Blade   Short Cup

1/2 cup of steamed or boiled green beans
1/2 cup of cooked brown rice
1/8 cup of water

1.) Add all ingredients to the *Short Cup* and twist on the *Baby Blend Blade*.
2.) Blend until you've achieved the proper consistency.
3.) Serve!

 Note – *Other great combinations to consider:*
Mango and Banana
Apples and Plums
Green Beans and Brown Rice
Pear and Millet
Apples and Oatmeal
Peas and Carrots
Yellow Squash and Brown Rice

 15 seconds

visit us on facebook

oatmeal cereal combos

Oatmeal is a wonderfully mild, comforting food that
works well in combination with both fruits and vegetables.
Great for both heart and immune system development, so
enjoy oatmeal often!

Milling Blade   Short Cup

1/2 cup of Whole Oats

4 cups of water

*1 cup of whole
oats yields 20
oz of stage one
baby food.*

1.) Add 1/2 cup of uncooked whole oats to the *Short Cup*.
2.) Twist on the *Milling Blade* and mill into a fine powder.
3.) Add the milled oatmeal and 4 cups of water to a pot
    and cover until it boils.
4.) Once it hits a boil, turn down heat to low and cook
    with cover on for 20 minutes.
5.) Test the consistency of the oatmeal cereal – if you
    want it thinner, add more water.
6.) Pour into a bowl and combine with your favorite fruit
    or veggie purée. (2 oz cereal w/2 oz fruit or veggie)
7.) Enjoy!

 Note – *This is a great cereal to combine with
any fruit or vegetable puree.*

 Tip – *Make combos with fresh ingredients,
or use two prepared purées and mix them
together!*

 30 seconds

*For more recipes, please visit
www.babybullet.com*

8 Months!

Even more flavors await your baby this month. Plus, it's a great time to start creating purées with a bit more texture to keep things interesting – and delicious! Simply add a bit less water and use the Pulse Technique on page 29 to find the right consistency for Baby. (If the new texture is not appreciated, simply add more water and blend Baby Bullet servings to create a smoother purée, then try the thicker texture a few days later.) Now that Baby has so many flavors to choose from, it's a great time to start **Batch Cooking**.

Even though Baby's digestive system is maturing, it's still VERY important to use the 4-day Food Introduction Schedule for <u>every single new food</u> that is introduced and track <u>any and all</u> reactions in the Food Journal.

Food Chart for Month 8

 =

1 Cup of Cantaloupe | 3 Baby Bullet servings (6 oz)
- **Don't Cook**

  =

2 Plums | 3.5 Baby Bullet servings (7 oz)

 =

1 Cup of Watermelon | 3 Baby Bullet servings (6 oz)
- **Don't Cook**

 =

1/3 Head of Cauliflower | 4 Baby Bullet servings (8 oz)

 =

1 Cup of Pineapple | 3 Baby Bullet servings (6 oz)
- **Don't Cook**

 =

1/3 Head of Broccoli | 6 Baby Bullet servings (12 oz)

 =

1 Cup Kale | 3 Baby Bullet servings (6 oz)

 =

1/2 of Eggplant | 6 Baby Bullet servings (12 oz)

 =

1 cup of turnip | 4 Baby Bullet servings (8 oz)

Note: *Fruit and vegetable sizes vary, so you may wind up with more or less food.*

Batch Cooking with Baby Bullet

This is where you really get to take advantage of all that the Baby Bullet has to offer, because now you can make 7 flavors of baby food in just about 5 minutes! Here is how to do it –

Choose your weekly menu and determine the quantities by using the Food Charts provided in each section and in your Pocket Nutritionist. Then, boil or steam all the fruits and vegetables in a big pot, so they cook at the same time.

If you've chosen any non-cook flavors, like banana, watermelon, canteloupe, pineapple or avocado… create those purées while the other flavors cook. They just need to be skinned, peeled, cored and/or seeded.

Then, peel, skin or core the fruits and vegetables (some skins come off easily after boiling or steaming) and add ¼ to ½ cup of water (water the produce boiled in is best because it has all the nutrients) and blend to the right texture. You can create up to 7 flavors in less than 5 minutes!

For foods you plan to serve within 3 days, refrigerate in either the *Short Cup* or in the *Storage Cups*. Use the *Date-Dial* to keep track of the preparation date. For freezing, either spoon into the *Batch Tray* or into the *Storage Cups* and freeze for up to 30 days.

Creating a week's worth of delicious, wholesome baby food has never been easier!

Feeding Schedule for Month 8

Time	Quantity	Drink
Wake Up Time	None	Breast/bottle
Breakfast	1 1/2 to 3 Baby Bullet servings	Breast/bottle
Lunch	1 1/2 to 3 Baby Bullet servings	Breast/bottle
Dinner	1 1/2 to 3 Baby Bullet servings	Breast/bottle
Bedtime	None	Breast/bottle

Foods: avocado, brown rice cereal, peas, zucchini, squash, apple, pear, banana, sweet potato, asparagus, carrots, green beans, white potato, peach, tofu, cottage cheese, milled oatmeal cereal, milled millet cereal, apricot, cantaloupe, plum, watermelon, broccoli, cauliflower, lentils, turnip, kale, eggplant, pineapple, greens.

Food groups: 4 - 5 servings of fruits and vegetables. 2 - 3 servings of cereal. 2 servings of protein.

Food consistency: Smooth purée - a little thicker than last month.

Stage One:
Perfect Thicker Purées

textured turnip

A great source of vitamin C, folic acid, calcium and magnesium, turnip makes a savory and satisfying purée that Baby will devour. To keep your turnip nice and thick, you'll use the Pulsing Technique on page 29.

Baby Blend Blade   Batchbowl

1 cup of well cooked, skinned turnip

¼ cup of water

. . . .

One cup of steamed, boiled or baked turnip (remove skin and greens) yields 8 oz of stage one baby food.

1.) Twist the *Baby Blend Blade* onto the bottom of the *Batchbowl*.
2.) Add both ingredients to the *Batchbowl* and secure the lid.
3.) Place the *Batchbowl* onto the *Power Base*.
4.) Press straight down on the cup very quickly and immediately release.
5.) Pulse the turnip a few times until you have a nice textured consistency.

 Note – *To make a thinner purée add more water and blend for a bit longer.*

 Tip! – *Use the Pulsing Technique (page 29) to create food with a more textured consistency.*

 Turnip and Brown Rice
It's like Thanksgiving dinner in a purée – these 2 flavors create a savory, satisfying meal you are sure to serve again and again.

 10 seconds

For more recipes, please visit
www.babybullet.com

peach and oatmeal

Rich in vitamin A, apricot is a very tasty way to promote good vision. Sweet and tangy, this purée is sure to be one of Baby's favorites!

Baby Blend Blade   Short Cup

1 cup of well cooked, pitted and peeled apricots

¼ cup of water

¼ cup of very cooked oatmeal

- -

1.) Add water and apricot to the *Short Cup*
2.) Twist on the *Baby Blend Blade*.
3.) Purée until you have achieved the proper smoothness.
4.) Spoon in cooked oatmeal until you achieve the right texture for Baby.

 Note – *To make a thinner purée add more water and blend for a bit longer.*

 Tip! – *Combine any fruit or vegetable with any cereal. Just be sure to use the 4 Day Food Introduction Schedule.*

 Apples and Oatmeal
Sure to be one of Baby's favorites! Simply combine a Baby Bullet serving of apple purée with a Baby Bullet serving of oatmeal cereal and get ready for some serious eating!!

 7 seconds

9 Months!
Stage Two - Tasty Textures

At this stage of Baby's development, it's time to thicken the meals up a bit. Start slow by adding well cooked rice, oatmeal or tiny pasta bits (stars are perfect) into purées. This adds a bit of texture and flavor. Stage 2 is a great time to start combining flavors as well. This will help you introduce more flavors and will help Baby develop a more mature palette.

During Stage 2 many wonderful foods can be introduced into Baby's diet. Chicken, red meat and shredded cheese... to name a few. Now that Baby has a much longer list of flavors to choose from, it's a great idea to make large batches of Baby Bullet servings in advance (see batch cooking page 70). That way, when a recipe calls for something like chicken – just throw in a thawed Baby Bullet serving of chicken – it couldn't be easier. It will save you an incredible amount of preparation time which allows you to be creative without spending too much time in the kitchen.

Stage 2 is a wonderful and fun time to start introducing finger foods such as cereal, tiny bits of fruit and minced pieces of vegetables.

Feeding Schedule for Month 9

Time	Food	Drink
Wake Up Time	None	Breast/bottle
Breakfast	1 1/2 to 3 Baby Bullet servings	Breast/bottle
Lunch	1 1/2 to 3 Baby Bullet servings	Breast/bottle
Dinner	1 1/2 to 3 Baby Bullet servings	Breast/bottle
Bedtime	None	Breast/bottle

Foods: avocado, brown rice cereal, peas, zucchini, squash, apple, pear, banana, sweet potato, asparagus, carrots, green beans, white potato, peach, tofu, cottage cheese, milled oatmeal cereal, milled millet cereal, apricot, cantaloupe, plum, watermelon, broccoli, cauliflower, beets, brussels sprouts, lentils, turnip, kale, eggplant, pineapple, greens, red meat, fish, turkey, beans, cheese.

Food groups: 4 - 5 servings of fruits and vegetables. 2 - 3 servings of cereal. 2 servings of protein.

Food consistency: Smooth purée - a little thicker than last month.

New Foods to Introduce!

Red Meat
Fish
Turkey
Black Beans
Kidney Beans
Garbanzos
Shredded Cheese
Whole Rice
Small/Well Cooked Pasta
Diced Veggies
Diced Fruits

Family Dinners
for Baby

chicken, brown rice squash

A tasty meal made of lean protein, complex carbs and nutrient rich fiber. What could be better? This is a meal you can cook for the whole family and then purée in the Baby Bullet for Baby's dinner or to store for later meals.

Baby Blend Blade   Batchbowl

One steamed/boiled yellow squash

½ cup of fully cooked chicken breast

½ cup of cooked brown rice

$1/8$ cup – ¼ cup of chicken or veggie broth

* If Baby is handling textures well, add the rice in AFTER puréeing.

. . . .

1.) Twist the *Baby Blend Blade* on to the bottom of the *Batchbowl*.
2.) Add the ingredients to the *Batchbowl* and secure the lid.
3.) Purée until you have achieved the proper smoothness.
4.) Enjoy or store.

 Note – *at this stage, thicker purées are better for your baby. But if Baby is having a hard time swallowing the thicker food – or keeps pushing the food out – stick with a thinner purée for a few more weeks.*

 10 seconds

turkey, rice and carrot

Delicious and nutritious, this is sure to become a favorite.

Baby Blend Blade   Batchbowl

One carrot steamed or boiled until soft

½ cup of fully cooked, diced turkey breast

½ cup of cooked rice (ideally brown)*

1 - 2 cups of chicken or veggie broth

* If Baby is handling textures well, add the rice in
    AFTER puréeing.

• •

1.) Twist the *Baby Blend Blade* on to the bottom of
    the *Batchbowl*.
2.) Add the ingredients to the *Batchbowl* and secure the lid.
3.) Purée until you have achieved the proper smoothness.
4.) Enjoy or store.

 Note – *at this stage, thicker purées are better
for your baby. But if Baby is having a hard time
swallowing the thicker food – or keeps pushing
the food out – stick with a thinner purée for a
few more weeks.*

 8 seconds

For more recipes, please visit
www.babybullet.com

10 - 12 Months!

At this point in Baby's development cycle, the single most efficient thing you can do is to create meals the WHOLE family can enjoy – even Baby! If your family is having pasta for dinner, simply spoon a properly sized portion into the Baby Bullet, add water and blend until you've achieved the proper consistency and serve for Baby as well! The more you can steer away from creating special baby meals, the more time you are going to have AWAY from the kitchen. Plus, any leftovers can go right in the Baby Bullet to get puréed, and stored in the refrigerator or freezer for another day.

Finger Foods

Finger foods and encouraging self-feeding are also very important once Baby has hit the 10-month mark. Provide Baby with a spoon at each meal and do your best to offer consistencies that are easy to get from bowl to mouth. Tiny bits of food that Baby can pinch between fingers should be provided at every meal. Cut up bits of fruit, beans and tiny pieces of pasta are great things to get right onto the high chair tray for easy access.

If your pediatrician approves, nuts including walnuts, cashews, almonds and nut butters can be a wonderful snack or meal. Easy to make and full of protein - you are going to go nuts with the nut butters!

Keep Introducing New Flavors

Once you pass the one-year mark, there is a good chance Baby will become a bit more finicky about trying new foods, so do your best to introduce a full spectrum of textures and flavors between the 10 and 12-month marks.

Now that Baby's dishes are a bit more sophisticated, it's a great idea to make a lot of Baby Bullet servings in advance. When you are armed with a freezer full of flavor – breakfast, lunch and dinner are a snap. So pick one or two days a week to whip up a few of Baby's favorites and store them in the freezer (see batch cooking page 70). Then, **when a recipe calls for something – just throw in a thawed Baby Bullet serving**. It will save you an incredible amount of preparation time and allows you to be creative without spending too much time in the kitchen.

Feeding Schedule for Months 10 - 12

Time	Food	Drink
Wake Up Time		Breast/bottle
Breakfast	3 - 4 Baby Bullet Servings	Breast/bottle
Lunch	3 - 4 Baby Bullet Servings	Breast/bottle
Snack	1 - 2 Baby Bullet Servings	Water
Dinner	3 - 4 Baby Bullet Servings	Breast/bottle
Bedtime		Breast/bottle

Foods: avocado, brown rice cereal, peas, zucchini, squash, apple, pear, banana, sweet potato, asparagus, carrots, green beans, white potato, peach, tofu, cottage cheese, milled oatmeal cereal, milled millet cereal, apricot, cantaloupe, plum, watermelon, broccoli, cauliflower, beets, brussel sprouts, lentils, turnip, kale, eggplant, pineapple, greens, nut butter, red meat, fish, turkey, beans, cheese.

Food groups: 4 - 5 servings of fruits and vegetables. 4 servings of grains, 2 - 3 servings of protein, 1 serving of dairy (1/2 cup yogurt or 1 oz of grated cheese).

Food consistency: Increase the chunkiness, plenty of finger foods.

Recipes for Months 10 - 12

petite pancakes

Perfect for the whole family, just cut up into the right sized bits for Baby and this one is sure to be a winner.

Baby Blend Blade

Batchbowl

1 cup whole wheat flour

3 tsp baking powder

1/2 tsp salt

1 tsp cinnamon

3/4 cup milk (or breast milk/formula)

1.) Twist on the *Baby Blend Blade* onto the bottom of the *Batchbowl*.
2.) Add all ingredients to the *Batchbowl* and secure the lid.
3.) Purée until you have achieved the proper smoothness.
4.) Spray a frying pan with olive oil and cook half dollar sized pancakes over medium heat until golden brown.

Pear Pancakes
Add 1 Baby Bullet serving of pear purée to the ingredients and blend. Yum!

Banana Pancakes
Add 2 Baby Bullet serving of banana purée (or ½ a banana) to the ingredients and blend. Yum!

 10 seconds

For more recipes, please visit
www.babybullet.com

minestrone

A fun and tasty soup with tons of flavor going on. This is a great one to make in big batches.

Baby Blend Blade

Batchbowl

1/3 cup green bean purée (or 1 Baby Bullet serving of green beans)

1/3 cup yellow squash purée (or 1 Baby Bullet serving of yellow squash)

1 cup of marinara sauce (or 3 Baby Bullet servings of marinara)

1 Tbs olive oil

1 clove of garlic (optional)

¼ cup of water

1 cup of cooked green bean bits

1 cup browned ground beef (or turkey)

½ cup cooked or canned kidney beans (no liquid)

1 cup of veggie broth

1 cup cooked mini-elbow pasta

· ·

1.) Add the first 6 ingredients to the *Batchbowl* and blend until smooth.
2.) Pour the contents into a sauce pan and cook over medium heat until heated through.
3.) Add in the beef, beans, broth, pasta and heat to desired temperature.
4.) Serve or store.

Serving Suggestion

Veggie Minestrone
Omit the ground beef from the recipe.

 14 seconds

For more recipes, please visit
www.babybullet.com

One Year +

What a difference a year makes! At this point of development, Baby's eating habits are becoming more like your own. Self-feeding with a spoon and picking up finger foods are skills that should be coming along swimmingly. Likes and dislikes of flavors and textures become more of an issue now that Baby can express emotions about what is on the menu.

At this one-year mark, it's more important than ever to make sure you provide a variety of healthy foods in all kinds of flavors and textures. This is the time when it's critical to set the foundation for a lifetime of healthy eating. In 6 months to a year, Baby is going to become quite finicky and if a new food is introduced during that window – good luck! They don't call them Terrible Twos for nothing! Variety is the spice of life, so don't fall into a rut of only providing Baby's favorites. Even if it goes untouched or it's just picked at, provide a cornucopia of foods so that they are, at the very least, familiar to your little one.

The First Year No-No List is now Yes-Yes!

Confirm with your pediatrician before offering any of the No-No foods (page 38) after Baby's first birthday, but there is a good chance you are going to get the green light on the following list.

Honey
Peanut Butter
Citrus Fruits
Raw Strawberries, Raspberries and Blackberries
Corn
Egg Whites
Whole Milk – as a drink
Wheat
Shellfish/Crustaceans

Because these foods are common allergens (hence having to wait so long to try them!) it's more important than ever to use your Food Journal and the 4-Day Food Introduction Schedule when introducing anything from the new Yes – Yes List.

Additionally, if there is a family history of allergies to any of these foods, feel free to wait a few more months to add them in. Allways consult your pediatrician for advice.

visit us on facebook

Food to Avoid Before 18 Months

Some foods are tougher to digest than others. And even though Baby's digestive system has come a long, long way…it's still developing. That being said, it's a good idea to avoid the following foods for another 6 months. At that time, check with your pediatrician to see if you can get a green light on:

Chocolate
Cabbage
Cucumbers
Vanilla
Onion (Raw)
Vanilla Flavoring

Adding "Puréed Goodness" To Everything You Make

Even though Baby is developing a more mature palette, there is no need to abandon purées yet!! Continue to make batches of Baby's favorite purées because **Baby Bullet servings are a super easy way to add nutrition to everything that Baby eats**. Plus, a lot of the recipes can be made in even LESS time when you use thawed Baby Bullet servings vs. starting from scratch. From macaroni and cheese with a touch of cauliflower purée to beef stew made from a base of carrot, tomato and yellow squash purée – Baby Bullet servings are going to save you time and money…again and again.

Recipes for
12 - 18 Months

stealth
scrambled eggs

An egg-ceptionally delicious and nutritious breakfast that can be made in seconds with the Baby Bullet! Your little one won't suspect a thing!

Baby Blend Blade   Short Cup

2 eggs

1 Baby Bullet serving of cauliflower purée (or zucchini)

¼ cup shredded cheese (optional)

. . . .

1.) Add all of the ingredients to the *Short Cup* and blend until smooth.
2.) Add a bit of cooking oil to the bottom of a frying pan and turn on medium heat.
3.) Pour egg mixture into the frying pan and stir with a spatula until the eggs are fluffy and full cooked.
4.) Serve immediately.

 14 seconds

For more recipes, please visit
www.babybullet.com

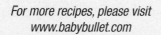

strawberry and pear totsicles

A sweet and healthy frozen treat for the whole family.

Baby Blend Blade

Short Cup

1 boiled pear (skinned and cored)

½ cup raw strawberries (remove tops)

¼ cup water

. . . .

1.) Add all of the ingredients to the *Short Cup* and blend until smooth.
2.) Use the Soft-Tip Spatula to spoon the ingredients into the Batch Tray.
3.) Fill as many cups as you can and then insert a plastic spoon into each filled cup. (use plastic wrap to keep in place)
4.) Freeze until hard like a pop.
5.) Serve and enjoy!

 10 seconds

For more recipes, please visit
www.babybullet.com

mac and cheese

Inevitably, macaroni and cheese will be one of your child's favorite foods. So, why not embrace the old mac and cheese and infuse it with some puréed goodness? This one's a keeper!

Baby Blend Blade   Short Cup

¼ cup of cheddar cheese

¼ cup ricotta cheese

1 Baby Bullet serving of yellow squash or cauliflower,

1 tsp butter

2-3 Tbs milk

1 cup cooked whole grain macaroni noodles.

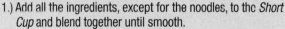

1.) Add all the ingredients, except for the noodles, to the *Short Cup* and blend together until smooth.
2.) Heat the cheese mixture in a saucepan over medium heat until melted and warm throughout.
3.) Toss into cooked macaroni noodles.

 8 seconds

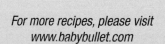

An exclusive offer for
baby bullet families!

Introducing the amazingly comprehensive baby food making bible...

the **baby bullet** recipe book and nutrition guide

Get <u>even more</u> out of your
baby bullet
with this soup to nuts baby food guide!

✔ Over 100 Nutrient Packed Recipes!

✔ Nutritional Facts for Each Flavor of Baby Food!

✔ Amazing Tips for Finicky Eaters!

✔ The Baking for Baby Section!

✔ Meal Ideas for Up to 3 Years!

✔ Toddler Friendly "Presentation" Tips!

✔ Healthy Dessert Recipes!

✔ Teething Biscuit Recipes... and More!

Visit
www.babybullet.com/bookoffer
or call
1-855-514-MYBB (1-855-514-6922)
to claim <u>your</u> special offer!

Food Journal

Date: _____

Foods Served: _____

_____

Time of Day Served: _____

Notes: _____

_____

_____

Date: _____

Foods Served: _____

_____

Time of Day Served: _____

Notes: _____

_____

_____

Date: _____

Foods Served: _____

_____

Time of Day Served: _____

Notes: _____

_____

_____

Date: _____

Foods Served: _____

_____

Time of Day Served: _____

Notes: _____

_____

_____

Food Journal

Date: _____

Foods Served: _____

_____

Time of Day Served: _____

Notes: _____

_____

_____

Date: _____

Foods Served: _____

_____

Time of Day Served: _____

Notes: _____

_____

_____

Date: _____

Foods Served: _____

_____

Time of Day Served: _____

Notes: _____

_____

_____

Date: _____

Foods Served: _____

_____

Time of Day Served: _____

Notes: _____

_____

_____

Food Journal

Date: _____

Foods Served: _____

_____

Time of Day Served: _____

Notes: _____

_____

_____

Date: _____

Foods Served: _____

_____

Time of Day Served: _____

Notes: _____

_____

_____

Date: _____

Foods Served: _____

_____

Time of Day Served: _____

Notes: _____

_____

_____

Date: _____

Foods Served: _____

_____

Time of Day Served: _____

Notes: _____

_____

_____

Food Journal

Date: _____

Foods Served: _____

_____

Time of Day Served: _____

Notes: _____

_____

_____

Date: _____

Foods Served: _____

_____

Time of Day Served: _____

Notes: _____

_____

_____

Date: _____

Foods Served: _____

_____

Time of Day Served: _____

Notes: _____

_____

_____

Date: _____

Foods Served: _____

_____

Time of Day Served: _____

Notes: _____

_____

_____

 # Food Journal

Date: _____

Foods Served: _____

_____

Time of Day Served: _____

Notes: _____

_____

_____

Date: _____

Foods Served: _____

_____

Time of Day Served: _____

Notes: _____

_____

_____

Date: _____

Foods Served: _____

_____

Time of Day Served: _____

Notes: _____

_____

_____

Date: _____

Foods Served: _____

_____

Time of Day Served: _____

Notes: _____

_____

_____

Food Journal

Date: _____

Foods Served: _____

_____

Time of Day Served: _____

Notes: _____

_____

_____

Date: _____

Foods Served: _____

_____

Time of Day Served: _____

Notes: _____

_____

_____

Date: _____

Foods Served: _____

_____

Time of Day Served: _____

Notes: _____

_____

_____

Date: _____

Foods Served: _____

_____

Time of Day Served: _____

Notes: _____

_____

_____

Food Journal

Date: _____

Foods Served: _____

_____

Time of Day Served: _____

Notes: _____

_____

_____

Date: _____

Foods Served: _____

_____

Time of Day Served: _____

Notes: _____

_____

_____

Date: _____

Foods Served: _____

_____

Time of Day Served: _____

Notes: _____

_____

_____

Date: _____

Foods Served: _____

_____

Time of Day Served: _____

Notes: _____

_____

_____

Food Journal

Date: _____

Foods Served: _____

_____

Time of Day Served: _____

Notes: _____

_____

_____

Date: _____

Foods Served: _____

_____

Time of Day Served: _____

Notes: _____

_____

_____

Date: _____

Foods Served: _____

_____

Time of Day Served: _____

Notes: _____

_____

_____

Date: _____

Foods Served: _____

_____

Time of Day Served: _____

Notes: _____

_____

_____

Food Journal

Date: _____

Foods Served: _____

_____

Time of Day Served: _____

Notes: _____

_____

_____

Date: _____

Foods Served: _____

_____

Time of Day Served: _____

Notes: _____

_____

_____

Date: _____

Foods Served: _____

_____

Time of Day Served: _____

Notes: _____

_____

_____

Date: _____

Foods Served: _____

_____

Time of Day Served: _____

Notes: _____

_____

_____

Food Journal

Date: _____

Foods Served: _____

_____

Time of Day Served: _____

Notes: _____

_____

_____

Date: _____

Foods Served: _____

_____

Time of Day Served: _____

Notes: _____

_____

_____

Date: _____

Foods Served: _____

_____

Time of Day Served: _____

Notes: _____

_____

_____

Date: _____

Foods Served: _____

_____

Time of Day Served: _____

Notes: _____

_____

_____

Food Journal

Date: _____

Foods Served: _____

_____

Time of Day Served: _____

Notes: _____

_____

_____

Date: _____

Foods Served: _____

_____

Time of Day Served: _____

Notes: _____

_____

_____

Date: _____

Foods Served: _____

_____

Time of Day Served: _____

Notes: _____

_____

_____

Date: _____

Foods Served: _____

_____

Time of Day Served: _____

Notes: _____

_____

_____

Food Journal

Date: _____

Foods Served: _____

_____

Time of Day Served: _____

Notes: _____

_____

_____

Date: _____

Foods Served: _____

_____

Time of Day Served: _____

Notes: _____

_____

_____

Date: _____

Foods Served: _____

_____

Time of Day Served: _____

Notes: _____

_____

_____

Date: _____

Foods Served: _____

_____

Time of Day Served: _____

Notes: _____

_____

_____

Food Journal

Date: _____

Foods Served: _____

_____

Time of Day Served: _____

Notes: _____

_____

_____

Date: _____

Foods Served: _____

_____

Time of Day Served: _____

Notes: _____

_____

_____

Date: _____

Foods Served: _____

_____

Time of Day Served: _____

Notes: _____

_____

_____

Date: _____

Foods Served: _____

_____

Time of Day Served: _____

Notes: _____

_____

_____

Food Journal

Date: _____

Foods Served: _____

_____

Time of Day Served: _____

Notes: _____

_____

_____

Date: _____

Foods Served: _____

_____

Time of Day Served: _____

Notes: _____

_____

_____

Date: _____

Foods Served: _____

_____

Time of Day Served: _____

Notes: _____

_____

_____

Date: _____

Foods Served: _____

_____

Time of Day Served: _____

Notes: _____

_____

_____

Food Journal

Date: _____

Foods Served: _____

_____

Time of Day Served: _____

Notes: _____

_____

_____

Date: _____

Foods Served: _____

_____

Time of Day Served: _____

Notes: _____

_____

_____

Date: _____

Foods Served: _____

_____

Time of Day Served: _____

Notes: _____

_____

_____

Date: _____

Foods Served: _____

_____

Time of Day Served: _____

Notes: _____

_____

_____

Food Journal

Date: _____

Foods Served: _____

_____

Time of Day Served: _____

Notes: _____

_____

_____

Date: _____

Foods Served: _____

_____

Time of Day Served: _____

Notes: _____

_____

_____

Date: _____

Foods Served: _____

_____

Time of Day Served: _____

Notes: _____

_____

_____

Date: _____

Foods Served: _____

_____

Time of Day Served: _____

Notes: _____

_____

_____

BABY BULLET ONE-YEAR LIMITED WARRANTY

At Baby Bullet, LLC, we take pride in our products. We go out of our way to make products of superior quality and craftsmanship, products designed to meet or exceed the demands placed on them through everyday use. Because of this commitment to quality, we warrant the Magic Bullet to be free of defects for one full year. Here's the deal: If your Magic Bullet stops operating to your satisfaction due to defects in materials or workmanship, we'll gladly repair it or replace it for free (excluding shipping and handling charges). For warranty service, simply call our customer service department @ **1-855-51-4-MYBB (1-855-514-6922)** or contact us via email from our website at www.babybullet.com, simply click the Customer Service link, fill out and submit the customer contact form and we will be glad to help you. At Baby Bullet, LLC, your complete satisfaction is our daily goal (hey, we know what it's like to be the customer!).

Baby Bullet, LLC warrants that the Baby Bullet is free of defects in materials and workmanship for one year from the date of purchase. This warranty is valid only in accordance with the conditions set forth below:

1. Normal wear and tear are not covered by this warranty. This warranty applies to consumer use only, and is void when the product is used in a commercial or institutional setting.

2. This warranty extends only to the original consumer purchaser and is not transferable. In addition, proof of purchase must be demonstrated. This warranty is void if the product has been subject to accident, misuse, abuse, improper maintenance or repair, or unauthorized modification.

3. This limited warranty is the only written or express warranty given by Baby Bullet, LLC. Any implied warranties on the product (including but not limited to any implied warranties of merchantability or fitness for a particular purpose) are limited in duration to the duration of this warranty. Some states do not allow limitations on how long an implied warranty lasts, so the above limitation may not apply to you.

4. Repair or replacement of the product (or, if repair or replacement is not feasible, a refund of the purchase price) is the exclusive remedy of the consumer under this warranty. Baby Bullet, LLC shall not be liable for any incidental or consequential damages for breach of this warranty or any implied warranty on this product. Some states do not allow the exclusion or limitation of incidental or consequential damages, so the above limitation or exclusion may not apply to you.

5. This warranty gives you specific legal rights, and you may also have other rights which vary from state to state.